AFRICAN
OPENINGS
TO THE TREE
OF LIFE

Compiled by
E. Peters, Scribe

Regent Press
1987

Library of Congress Cataloging-in-Publication Data

Peters, Erskine.
   African openings to the tree of life.

   "An expanded version of . . . Developing the inner
self" - - T.p. verso.
   Includes bibliographies.
   1. Spiritual life. 2. Africa, Sub-Saharan - -
Religion. I. Peters, Erskine. Developing the inner
self. II. Title
BL624.P475   1987   299'.6   87-6017
ISBN 0-916147-06-1

African Openings to the Tree of Life
is an expanded version of the earlier book
Developing the Inner Self:
Meditations Based Upon African Wisdom

Second Printing, October 1990
Third Printing, January 1994
Fourth Printing, January 1996

Manufactured in the United States of America
Regent Press
6020-A Adeline
Oakland, California 94608

You got a right, I got a right,
We all got a right to the tree of life.

The very time I thought I was lost,
The dungeon shook and the chain fell off.

— from James Weldon and
J. Rosamond Johnson,
*The Books of American
Negro Spirituals*
(Viking Press)

If we open our eyes,
We may see;
If we share the light of our vision,
We may give a pointer to immortality.

FORWARD

These life principles have been abstracted and extracted from African philosophy, religion, mythology, folklore, rituals, and symbolism. These principles pertain to total development. They may relate on different levels to the person, the family, the social group, the spiritual group, the neighborhood, the community, or work organization.

These principles are intended to orient one toward understanding, seeing, and living life as an on-going process. The principles may be used to deal with, or simply reflect upon life in its many aspects. Certain principles presented here, when turned over in the mind, or worked with meditatively, for example, may provide solutions to a vast range of problems.

Principles by their very nature are manifold in their dimensions just as life in its essence is manifold in dimension. These African principles are expected to hold within them the power of life—and life over death. Thus, it is not intended that one simply accept the principles but that one use them.

Some users will need and reflect on certain principles at times more than they will need or reflect on others. But needs change as life changes, and growth is an engaging process which, while it uses energy also brings or creates energy. It is important to remember though that growth does lead one into transitions and that transitions are not always easy. Transitions are often, however, tests of our preparation for growth. One may find that the same principles which have helped lead one into transition may also need to be used to lead one out.

Life is a dynamic process, and by our own means we partake of that process. Sometimes these principles may work quite instantly; sometimes they may take months or years to bring us into new light. Their effectiveness requires varying degrees of personal effort. Timing of their efficacy depends on effort and circumstance. But when one is ready, one moves.

* * *

* * *

Realizing and attaining the magnificent within ourselves is a creative process. It is a movement through eternity which makes every person a voyager. However, all voyagers are not sure of the course. Some wander eternally, which may be what hell is, but others make use of charts, compasses, and lighthouses — life-principles. The journey moves toward alignment of the personal with the cosmic. Through alignment with the cosmic, the person seeks to fulfill the ultimate in self-esteem by feeling or realizing her or his divinity. The insightful voyager, then, perceives time as a matter of degrees of being in or out of alignment with the Ultimate Source, as a matter of degrees before being made whole.

Trials are a part of the grammar of human experience. The only way to overcome and understand trials is by growing more in line with the divine self, and to do the best one can against the odds. Through alignment with the divine aspect of the self, we may comprehend more of the causes of trials.

Bondages of perception or certain frames of illusion cause us to put our emphases on mis-proportioning ourselves, rather than upon being, realizing, and creating ourselves. Through divine alignment, however, one learns to oversee the situation, rather than have the situation oversee him or her.

By the light of the priests and priestesses, the knowledge-holders of the great principles, we can be led out of the bondages of perception. By the light of the knowledge-holders we begin to understand how not to mistake a thing for its essence. We begin to learn as well that the cosmos is all one existence, made one by the permeation of energy, and that material is really energy given shape. This is the voyage of knowledge, however, that each one must take.

May you find the voyage both invigorating and productive. The charters, the priests and priestesses, the knowledge-holders, are waiting.

I

They who cannot confess their limitation to the Divine Head cannot begin the process of fulfillment, say the knowledge-holders.

They who are not willing to sacrifice will not be fulfilled, say the knowledge-holders. Sacrifice harmonizes through right measure, it realigns forces, say the knowledge-holders.

The human being's freedom is in the inner head, say the knowledge-holders.

AFRICAN OPENINGS

Human beings shape their destinies according to the relationship between the outer and inner head, say the knowledge-holders.

It is the human being's inner head which brings relief, say the knowledge-holders. The human being should consult first the inner-head, say the knowledge-holders. The inner head will lead the human being to the proper source.

Only the inner head will accompany a devotee on a long journey without turning back, say the knowledge-holders.

True doorways are strict, say the knowledge-holders.

For human beings to receive blessings they must be in consent with receiving them, say the knowledge-holders.

When the inner head prescribes and the human being subscribes, the tree bears fruit say the knowledge-holders.

Neglect of duty to self, brother, or sister creates spiritual imbalance, say the knowledge-holders. Neglect is the empowering of imperfection. Imperfection is an attacker in many forms, the greatest safeguard against which is the inner head, say the knowledge-holders.

The inner head does not like to be slighted, say the knowledge-holders.

Various imperfections eclipse human beings from the full light of the First Source, say the knowledge-holders. Blindness devours reason. Blindness finds trouble recognizing the healer, say the knowledge-holders. Sore are the eyes of the blind and they fear touching. Sore are the owners, who do not know up from down and must be coaxed by the breaker of the seal, say the knowledge-holders.

One person's eyes may be made of another person's mouth, say the knowledge-holders.

Immortality is the inheritance of the partakers of Great Wisdom, say the knowledge-holders.

Great seeing and good speaking cause the raising of the dead and the reassembling of the dismembered and move them toward the First Source, say the knowledge-holders; which leads to heaven in the soul and brings rebirth.

The Divine loves humanity and has filled it with its sight so that humanity might see how to be joined with the Divine, say the knowledge-holders, and to conquer all enemies. The sacred laws have been formulated for salvation, and for support of humanity, say the knowledge-holders.

The dead are not resurrected without embrace, say the knowledge-holders, which is the sharing principle.

Freedom comes by alignment with the First Source, for by that light human beings see best how to choose, say the knowledge-holders.

Sight and creation always interact, say the knowledge-holders.

One who is equipped never trembles, the knowledge-holders say.

The words of earth are spoken to heaven and are weighed there, the knowledge-holders say. Upon words is the seat made in the head.

The flame of the fire of blessedness comes to those who gather about the throne of blessedness, the knowledge-holders say.

True seekers of Wisdom use the Divine formula, the Divine equation of ever knocking and ever asking. Nothing is denied those ever using the Divine formula and equation of proper knocking and proper asking, say the knowledge-holders.

Existence has a face on every side and every face teaches a lesson. Those who fully understand existence do not separate the faces from the lessons, say the knowledge-holders. Every lesson reveals aspects of Cosmic Law.

The human being has its structure from the Temple of Wisdom. Human beings should learn to read their own scroll. In it is written the key to Cosmic Law, say the knowledge-holders. The human body epitomizes on earth Cosmic Function. Every aspect of creation bears the stamp of Cosmic Law, say the knowledge-holders.

Only consciousness brings ascendency, say the knowledge-holders.

In nakedness is best-seeing, feeling, hearing, thinking, smelling, tasting, say the knowledge-holders. And every face is an illusion which consciousness burns away. The child is not ashamed of nakedness, say the knowledge-holders.

All the passions — fear, envy, pride, greed, sloth, lust, and anger — are opposed to consciousness, say the knowledge-holders.

Blessed is the person that learns the Law for the sake of the Law, say the knowledge-holders.

Blessed are the persons who are their own discipline, say the knowledge-holders. And blessed are those who know that gifts can bring chaos or peace, according to their use. Blessed is the person in whom freedom awakens conscience, say the knowledge-holders.

Put wisdom to work and evil will flee you, say the knowledge-holders. Respect for the Law yields virtue; disrespect yields limitation, the knowledge-holders say.

Rightness is the love of the First Source and the First Source is in love with rightness, say the knowledge-holders.

The secret to opening every door is in its bolt, say the knowledge-holders. The bolt prescribes the exact medium.

In the original name is the original essence, say the knowledge-holders.

The true temple is the holding place of Cosmic Law, say the knowledge-holders.

Helplessness stems from the ignorance of errors, but consciousness attracts the power of the Law, say the knowledge-holders.

Obedience itself is bowing, say the knowledge-holders. It is the humbling of the heart.

Because the human being is spirit, the human being may communicate with spirit, say the knowledge-holders.

Because spirit is imperishable, the human being is imperishable, say the knowledge-holders. Time stamps the spirit's qualities.

Discipline is the conservation of the gifts of the First Source, say the knowledge-holders.

Sin is really limitation, say the knowledge-holders. It is unwholeness, separation from the First Source which is full presence of knowledge, power, place and time, say the knowledge holders.

Say the knowledge-holders, evil is a force fearing conversion.

Initiation teaches perpetual initiation, say the knowledge-holders.

II

THE
POTENT
CENTER

If a man says yes, the
Spirit says yes.
— Ibo

Say the knowledge-holders, right reward stems from right and just speaking and thinking, right desire and right possession, right regard of nuturers, right use of self and others, and right relation to whole.

Say the knowledge-holders, the best life is achieved by engagement with systematic process. The best life is built on systematic use of life-giving principles.

Say the knowledge-holders, all vibrates around the center, all proceeds from the center, all can get power, illumination, and life from the center.

19

To stay in focus, to keep on base, to maintain poise, say the knowledge-holders, to be erect, keep association with the center. The life-charge proceeds from the center.

Say the knowledge-holders, persons off base with the center cannot identify themselves.

Say the knowledge-holders, persons off base with the center cannot chart themselves.

At the center everything crosses; and in crossing is creative force. Everything created crosses, say the knowledge-holders. Dissociation from the center is foolishness, say the knowledge-holders.

Say the knowledge-holders, that which is not centered tears apart, but what is centered is coherent.

Say the knowledge-holders, centering leads to self-knowing. Self-knowing is the dynamic of destiny, say the knowledge-holders. The relation to the center is the guide for the self. The center is the reflector for the self, say the knowledge-holders.

The center is the stone of faith, say the knowledge-holders. Recognition of the center labels self-confidence. Doubt of the center marks the imperfected. A person would be foolish not to contact the center, say the knowledge-holders.

Say the knowledge-holders, the center opens forth for the imperfected. The part becomes whole at the center, say the knowledge-holders.

Say the knowledge-holders, there is truly no expanding without centering. A person is foolish not to contact the center, say the knowledge-holders.

There is no aligning without centering, say the knowledge-holders. Messages cannot be sent without centering.

Centering opens other eyes, say the knowledge-holders. Centering is awakening.

The uncentered self cannot agree on its direction. It is weak in force, say the knowledge-holders.

The uncentered self has given in to outer force, say the knowledge-holders. It sends worship in the wrong direction.

At the center is the great time-keeper, where is also the power for judging and measuring, say the knowledge-holders.

Say the knowledge-holders, one who does not use the life-giving principles is foolish.

The Potent Center is conglomerate force, say the knowledge-holders.

The way to the Source is in rightness of heart, but the way is not always straight, say the knowledge-holders.

III

SUPPLICATION

Unless you call out, who
will open the door?
— Ethiopia

Supplication is a manner of opening up to power, say the knowledge-holders.

Say the knowledge-holders, supplication is confirmation of the Supreme Resource.

Right supplication brings honor to the tongue and to the ear. It is reverberation, sending and receiving, say the knowledge-holders. Right praying is right listening, say the knowledge-holders.

Right supplication is not for oneself, but for oneness, say the knowledge-holders. It is connecting in order to center.

Say the knowledge-holders, supplication is adoration of the Greater but raising of the smaller. It is kneeling to heighten.

Say the knowledge-holders, bowing is washing.

IV

THE
EXERCISE
OF
SACRIFICE

Farmers hoe and hoe; they
forget not one weed on
yam heaps.
— Yoruba

One cannot both feast
and become rich.
— Ashanti

Sacrifices have to be made to stay toward the center,
say the knowledge-holders.

If what is to be offered is not one's own, then how can
it be a sacrifice, say the knowledge-holders? What is
precious is given up for something more precious, say
the knowledge-holders.

What does not strengthen should be released, for it is
a false treasure, say the knowledge-holders.

Say the knowledge-holders, sacrifice opens doors. No true entering is done without sacrifice.

When one puts forth one takes in, say the knowledge-holders.

Say the knowledge-holders, loving cannot be done without sacrifice; thus linking is not made without sacrifice.

Say the knowledge-holders, the motive of the sacrifice must be as great as the object.

Say the knowledge-holders, the good of the object signifies the good of the motive of the sacrifice.

Sacrifice marks the consciousness, say the knowledge-holders.

V

ESTABLISHING
LIFE
THROUGH
KNOWLEDGE
OF
THE
ENERGIES

He who cannot dance will
say: "The drum is bad."
— Ashanti

A fool and water will go
the way they are diverted.
— Ethiopia

To make preparations does
not spoil the trip.
— Guinea

Human beings are related, like everything else, to everything else, to every other part of creation, that is, to
every other aspect of the cosmos. Energy is always
alive, radiating, and vibrating to some degree. All existence interacts and is interconnected by this activity
of energies, say the knowledge-holders.

A person is made of energy, not of material, say the
knowledge-holders. Terrible things begin to happen
when the person is seen as material; for all is a network,
say the knowledge-holders.

33

Say the knowledge-holders, all existence is cosmic energy, all energy vibrates, all energy is connected.

Say the knowledge-holders, what is perceived as material is a cosmic energy form.

Energy is the force of life, say the knowledge-holders.

Energy brings distinction to matter, say the knowledge-holders.

The child seen as material cannot be raised, say the knowledge-holders.

The child seen as material is denied life, say the knowledge-holders.

Mastery puts the harness to energy; mastery puts value to energy, say the knowledge-holders.

Inclination is the indication of energy. Say the knowledge-holders, determination is the force of energy.

The laws of creation work by the conversion of energy,
say the knowledge-holders.

VI

ESTABLISHING
LIFE
THROUGH
LIFE'S
RHYTHMS

It is danced and a chance
is given to others.
— Zulu

Energy flows in stages and cycles, say the knowledge-holders.

Birth is always the emergence of energy, say the knowledge-holders. Spirit emerges at birth.

Say the knowledge-holders, each phase must be seen as preparation for another phase.

Each phase unattended jeopardizes another phase, say the knowledge-holders.

Consciousness itself is preparation, say the knowledge-holders.

Say the knowledge-holders, consciousness is potency.

Say the knowledge-holders, childhood is the phase for discovery of energy, for the naming of energy.

Say the knowledge-holders, childhood is the phase for the guiding of energy, for the first preparation for the use of energy.

Say the knowledge-holders, initiation is the lure to mastery.

Puberty may be like a swinging bridge if not given the lure to mastery, say the knowledge-holders.

The adult phase marks responsibility, say the knowledge-holders, a greater level of mastery.

Marriage is unity for making, say the knowledge-holders. In making is the power of energy.

Say the knowledge-holders, aging is not dying but coming to seed.

Say the knowledge-holders, death is always a signal for birth.

Say the knowledge-holders, in rituals are life formulae.

Say the knowledge-holders, in life is experience for wisdom. This makes time a matter of degree if one understands one's own clock, say the knowledge-holders.

VII

Awake out of thy sufferings,
O thou who liest prostrate!
Awake thou!
Thy head is in the horizon.
—THE BOOK OF THE DEAD

Say the knowledge-holders, only the liar testifies to the origin of Creative Being.

Say the knowledge-holders, the broken covenant kills the friend.

Say the knowledge-holders, it is the stick of discipline that leads.

Say the knowledge-holders, when enough is understood, death is conquered.

Say the knowledge-holders, disease is chaotic, healing is order.

Say the knowledge-holders, true home is the place from which the sun breaks.

Say the knowledge-holders, right practice is true knowing.

Say the knowledge-holders, a vow is an obligation for which payment must be made.

Say the knowledge-holders, the way will be made open for them that have power over their feet, which is power over their understanding.

Say the knowledge-holders, let shame come over those who would hinder the rising of the dead.

Say the knowledge-holders, love openeth all the ways. Spirit enters into closed places.

Say the knowledge-holders, the mouth of truth shall overwhelm evil.

AFRICAN OPENINGS

*   *   *

The cleaned heart carries no weight, say the knowledge-holders.

They that find the frontier and that make themselves invisible shall rise into the crown of wisdom, say the knowledge-holders. For they that live for life never die.

*   *   *

SOURCES
TO
THE
KNOWLEDGE
HOLDERS

Abimbola, 'Wande. *Ifá: An Exposition of Ifá Literary Corpus.* Ibadan: Oxford University Press Nigeria, 1976.

Abimbola, 'Wande. *Ifa Divination Poetry.* New York: Nok 1977.

Adler, Alfred and Zempléni, Andrao. *Le baton de l'aveugle. Divination, maladie et pouvoir chez les Moudang du Tchad.* Paris: Hermann, 1972.

Arinze, F. A. *Sacrifice in Iba Religion.* Ibadan: Ibadan University Press, 1970.

Awoonor, Kofi. *Guardians of the Sacred Word: Ewe Poetry.* New York: Nok, 1974.

Bakari, Mtoro bin Mwinyi. *The Customs of the Swahili People.* Berkeley: Univeristy of California Press, 1981.

Balandier, Georges and Jacques Maquet. *Dictionary of Black African Civilization.* New York: Leon Amiel, 1974.

Biebuyck, D. and Kahombo, C. Mateene. *The Mwindo Epic.* Berkeley and Los Angeles: The University of California Press, 1971.

Budge, E. A. Wallis. *The Book of the Dead.* New York: Bell Publishing Company, 1960.

Budge, E. A. Wallis. *Osiris and the Egyptian Resurrection,* Vols. I & II. New York: Dover Publications, 1973.

Byaruhanga—Akiiki, A. B. T. (Compiler). *Occasional Research Papers on African Religions and Philosophies.* Kampala: Makerere University. 20 vols. From 1971 - June 1974.

Danguah, J. B. *The Akan Doctrine of God.* London: Frank Cass and Company Ltd, 1968.

de Lubicz, Isha Schwaller. *Her-Bak: The Living Face of Ancient Egypt.* Vol. I. New York: Inner Traditions International Ltd., 1978.

de Lubicz, Isha Schwaller. *Her-Bak: Egyptian Initiate,* Vol. II. New York: Inner Traditions International Ltd., 1978.

Ezeanya, S. N. "The Place of the Supreme God in the Traditional Religion of the Igbo," *West African Religion*, Vol. I, 1963, pp. 1-4.

Griaule, Marcel. *Conversations With Ogotemmêli: An Introduction to Dogon Religious Ideas.* London: Oxford University Press for the International African Institute, 1965.

Idowu, E. B. *African Traditional Religion.* London: S. C. M. Press, 1973.

RESOURCES TO THE KNOWLEDGE HOLDERS

Idowu, E. B. *Olódùmarè: God in Yoruba Belief.* London: Longmans, Green and Company Ltd., 1966.

Kimambo, I. N. and C. K. Omari. "The Development of Religious Thought and Centres Among the Pare." In Ranger, T. O. and Kimambo, I. N. (eds.), *The Historical Study of African Religion.* Berkeley: University of California Press, 1972, pp. 111-121.

Koech, Kipng'eno. "African Mythology: a Key to Understanding African Religion." In *African Religions: A Symposium.* ed. N. S. Booth. New York: Nok Publishers, Ltd., 1977, pp. 117-139.

Leslau, Charlotte and Peter. *African Proverbs.* Mount Vernon: Peter Pauper Press, 1962.

Lienhardt, Godfrey. *Divinity and Experience: The Religion of the Dinka.* Oxford: The Clarendon Press, 1967.

Mainga, Mutumba. "A History of Lozi Religion to the End of the Nineteenth Century." In Ranger, T. O. and Kimambo, I. N. (eds)., *The Historical Study of African Religion.* Berkeley: University of California Press, 1972, pp. 95-107.

Mbiti, John S. *African Religions and Philosophy.* New York: Doubleday Anchor Books, 1970.

Mbiti, John S. *The Prayers of African Religions.* New York: Orbis Books, 1976.

Mendonsa, Eugene L. "Etiology and Divination Among the Sisala of Northern Ghana." *Journal of Religion in Africa,* Vol. IX fascicule 1, (1978) pp. 33-50.

Mercier, Jacques. *Ethiopian Magic Scrolls.* New York: George Braziller, 1979.

M'Timkulu, Donald. "Some Aspects of Zulu Religion." In *African Religions: A Symposium.* ed. N. S. Booth. New York: Nok Publishers, Ltd., 1977, 13-30.

Nketia, J. H. B. *African Gods and Music.* Legon: Institute of African Studies, Univeristy of Ghana, 1970.

Ocholla-Ayayo, A. B. C. *Traditional Ideology and Ethics Among the Southern Luo.* Uppsala: Scandinavian Institute of African Studies, 1976.

Ubah, C. N. "The Supreme Being, Divinities and Ancestors in Igbo Traditional Religion: Evidence From Otanchara and Otanzu." *Africa: Revue de l'Institut Africain International.* Vo. 52, no. 2 (1982), 90-105.

Wanjohi, G. J. "An African Conception of God: The Case of the Gikuyu." *Journal of Religion in Africa,* Vol. IX, fascicule 2 (1978), 136-146.

Zuesse, Evan M. "Action as the Way of Transcendence: The Religious Significance of the Burami Cult of the Lega." *Journal of Religion in Africa,* Vol. IX, fascicule 1 (1978), pp. 62-72.

VIII

THE
WAY
OF
IDEAS
AND
SYMBOLS

*

The sayings of the knowledge-holders have been transmitted over the ages through ideas and symbols.

Ideas and symbols have power and energy. There are ways, systems, or manners by which ideas and symbols serve as manifestations, configurations, and stimulators of power and energy.

*

Ideas and symbols are in their own way living phenomena. They are conceived, they gestate, they are born, they mature, and they die. Some lie dormant for thousands of years and then are resurrected.

Cultures and civilizations are built upon and around ideas and symbols.

*

Ideas and symbols are not pure sources within themselves. They are points of culmination. This is true of the negatively created ones, too. Humans as dynamic, thinking beings eventually challenge all ideas and symbols, thereby demolishing or recreating and reconstructing them toward new points.

*

Symbols often appeal more to the intuition than do ideas. Yet symbols and ideas rely upon both the intuitive and the rational to some degree. Ideas often seem more explicit, but like symbols they too rely upon coding and encoding as functional knowledge constructs and as forms of communication.

Though confounding they may sometimes be, symbols and ideas propose clarifications. For in their most positive sense, they work to communicate essences.

*

New and old ideas and symbols balance and counterbalance. They create peace or flux. Ideas and symbols are never asleep within themselves. When people change aspects of their identity, for example, some idea is symbolized in whatever new aspect they may have taken on.

*

Ideas and symbols can focus and compel the work-
ing of the intellect. Being engaged with them may
make one feel the distinction of the species as well as
feel the species' affinity to the Divine.

*

Ideas contain, project, and transmit energy. Con-
versely, they may stifle energy. Ideas determine atti-
tudes. Ideas determine destiny.

Acting as stimuli ideas may cause mental reactions
that can be traced and sensed physiologically. Presented under appropriate conditions, ideas can cause
one's energy to rise or fall. A simple idea attacking
one's self-esteem can make one's energy level fall. It
takes an idea as powerful to make it rise again. This is
much of the way of ideas.

*

Ideas are constructs and approximations of truth as
we think we apprehend it. Ideas are constructs by
which we may be prompted to investigate the nature
of the real. Ideas are configurations functioning to

connect and articulate thoughts or images.

*

Veritable ideas engage us in process and lead into generation. Veritable ideas suggest formulated, compelling thought. They may grow out of notions and inklings but do not remain so. They have a communicable or apprehensible logic, which for our intelligence is, when crystalline, virtually self-validating and demonstrable.

*

People embracing ideas expect rewards, or apprehend the rewards at the moment of embrace—practical, material, spiritual. Perhaps we do not always expect the same from symbols but since symbols, too, contain ideas, being in actuality the graphic representation of ideas, we may expect the same.

Ideas are breeding grounds. While we are not always so easily inclined to embrace change itself, we are more readily inclined to embrace change when the ideas prompting the change are associated with appreciable and perceivable rewards. Indeed the ardor with which we struggle with ideas is the result of the anticipated outcome.

*

Even more influential is the idea which carries within it the capacity for imbuing personal autonomy, self-esteem, or human enjoyment. The same idea may stimulate the physical in some or the metaphysical in others, of course, since all ears will not register the same words in the same way.

*

What is generally expected from ideas is some form of liberation. In the excitement of the discovery of new and potent ideas, we often expect total liberation.

*

People are constantly in need of new ideas since life is full of issues. Some people discover a few seminal ideas which they use to direct their lives and solve or mediate most of the issues by which they are confronted. Many others are not always so lucky. Yet, they, too, stand on the look out for that particular idea, or those ideas, which they feel may provide an appropriate index for managing and understanding their existence.

*

Symbols too may serve this function without our understanding why. A combination of lines or colors, for instance, can have varying effects. The effects can vary from person to person. That which brings peacefulness to one may bring confusion to another.

*

It is ideas that cause evolution and revolution: ideas in their proper timing, phrasing, and setting. Since it is the nature of ideas to compel and challenge, it is the way of ideas to first effect change of mind.

*

Considering people as existing somewhat in inert, latent, and active states—if we were to match up these states with aspects of or elements involved in nuclear fission, that is, atomic particles; and if we were to match these states up with what happens to cause nuclear fission, we might say that an idea under proper conditions can act upon a human to set off energy and activity in the same way that a neutron, when it bombards the atom, similarly releases an energy field.

The inert mind may be very much like the least volatile of elements. Even so, there is a tremendous force at the heart of its structure that makes it inert; but a reversal of that same energy force that makes it inert, by coming into contact with the proper idea under the proper conditions, could cause a mighty explosion.

The more active mind may be very much like uranium, one of the most volatile of the elements, more easily setting off an explosion or releasing energy when struck by the neutron. And the more active mind obviously responds more readily when aptly struck by an idea.

*

Ideas can be food for intellect, body, and spirit. Some are very palatable, some less. Some are very digestible, some less. As with food, so it is with ideas that we do not always eat what we need. The immediacy of desire often holds precedence until we come to acknowledge that bad ideas bring bad returns, until we develop the skill for recognizing the more useful ideas from the rather useless ones.

*

An idea overstated is as useless as an idea oversimplified. For that reason, thinkers yearn to phrase their thoughts as pure crystals. While the thinker hopes for us to use his thoughts to see, the thinker also desires that we be able to see through the thoughts. Part of the potency and vitality of ideas is that they have this quality of reciprocity.

*

Symbols are among the most economical of communicative forms. They often accompany ideas in the form of emblems. They function so very economically that they can become like language concentrate, which is what makes their meaning so obscure when their codes are not available or are simply lost.

*

Manifold in meaning, implication, ramification, though by nature coherent and unified, symbols bring together thoughts, images, and ideas as the Greek roots *syn* (together) and *ballein* (to throw) suggest.

*

A symbol stands for something else, something beyond itself, beyond its literal depiction. It stands for a meaning its creator wants to capture or communicate. It is a form into which thought is projected.

*

Symbols have reciprocative power. They take on or take in meaning as well as give off meaning. Of course, the meaning is determined by what is lodged in the perceiving consciousness, which consequently leads to or becomes point of view.

Symbols are indices. Because they are integrated information images, they reveal by association.

The symbol is never one particular thing. It is always suggestive of what particular things can connote when placed in patterns or associations.

*

That the symbol generally conceals as much as it reveals is testimony to how it can function as *process*. The mind wishing to unveil the concealed becomes engaged with the form. The consciousness connects with the form, and through this binding process revelation is possible. Thus, connecting is requisite to knowing. On some level we must engage the symbol if we are to know it.

*

The personal world itself is full of symbolic value: domestic, linguistic, etc.

*

Like the idea, the symbol can be viewed from more than one side. It can be converted to more than one side, more than one use. Its intended use does not always determine its use.

*

People who understand power always understand the power of ideas and symbols. In order to reduce the power of symbols, we have to de-mystify them. In order to do this we have to have the power to show the symbol as vulnerable by distortion, assault, or usurpation—providing that the assumed power is actually in the configuration of ideas associated with it.

Our ignorance of how symbols hold power is for certain one of the major reasons they often hold power over us. Not unexpectedly then symbols are frequently intimidating. The same is true of ideas.

*

Since it is the way of symbols to support ideas, new ideas must demonstrate their force not only always in contention with the challenged ideas but often, too, with the challenged ideas' symbols. Sometimes the destruction of the symbol coincides with the challenge made to the established idea as with, for example, the French revolutionists in their storming the Bastille, both literally and symbolically seizing and destroying the stored power. At other times symbols simply fall by the wayside, having lost the creditable backing of ideas.

*

Ideas and symbols represent discriminations, categories. These may not always be positive in motive or effect. In their greatest sense, however, ideas and symbols work toward the exercise of the mind, of the spirit: of being. In their greatest form they do not allow stagnation because they promote continuous generation. This is the true exercise pointed to by yoga, for instance.

*

Ideas are made to fill voids. They attempt ultimately to fill the void of human knowledge.

The Ancient Egyptians held that things are the reflection of archetypal or eternal ideas so great in scope that our human minds do not yet possess the sophistication or magnitude to apprehend fully these archetypal or eternal ideas in their true essence. We are only capable of grasping a reflection and not even all of that, they held, especially if we attempt to apply too much human analysis. In this acknowledgement they constructed a system of hieroglyphs—symbolic ideas expressing simultaneously a degree of knowledge apprehended as well as expressing the ineffability of total knowledge. Nevertheless they found the degrees they apprehended, if not fulfilling, certainly stimulating.

*

In its own special way, engagement with ideas and symbols can be the elixir of life. Following ideas and symbols may, because it can become an eternal process of alternation and generation, be the way or road to immortality itself.

*

RESOURCES
FOR
FURTHER
READING

Cirlot, Juan Edwardo, *A Dictionary of Symbols.* London: Routledge and Kegan Paul, 1973.

Colton, Ann Ree. *Watch Your Dreams: A Master Key and Reference Book For All Initiates of the Soul, the Mind, and the Heart.* Glendale: ARC Publishing Company, 1979.

Ferguson, George. *Signs and Symbols in Christian Art.* New York: Oxford University Press, 1974.

Jung, Carl Gustav (ed.). *Man and His Symbols.* New York: Dell Publishing Company, 1973.

Jung, Carl Gustav. *Psyche and Symbol.* ed. Violet de Laszlo. Garden City: Doubleday Anchor Books, 1958.

Murry, Henry A. (ed.). *Myth and Mythmaking.* Boston: Beacon Press, 1960.

Schwaller de Lubicz, R. A. *Symbol and the Symbolic: Egypt, Science and the Evolution of Consciousness.* Brookline: Autumn Press Books, 1978.

Silberer, Herbert. *Hidden Symbolism of Alchemy and the Occult Arts.* New York: Dover Publications, Inc., 1971.

About the Author

Erskine Peters is a graduate of Paine College (Augusta, Georgia), where he majored in English with a minor in Philosophy and Religion. He also studied at Oberlin College and Yale University. He earned the Ph.D. in English from Princeton University, and has taught at the University of California/Berkeley and at UCLA. Presently, he is Professor of English and Black Studies at the University of Notre Dame.

Professor Peters is also the author of *William Faulkner: The Yoknapatawpha World and Black Being* (1983), published by Norwood/Folcroft Editions, Darby, Pennsylvania, and *Fundamentals of Essay Writing: An Orientation Manual* (1987), Regent Press, Oakland, California. He is also author of the forthcoming *Lyrics of the Afro-American Spiritual* (Greenwood Press) and *The New Millenium: Afro-American Destiny and the Twenty-First Century* (Regent Press).

ORDER FORM

To receive copies of *African Openings to the Tree of Life* by mail, send $12.95 per book. This price includes postage and handling ($9.95 + $3.00). California residents please add 8.25% sales tax. Discounts are available for larger orders. Please inquire.

I am enclosing a : ❏ money order   or   ❏ check in the amount of $ _____ to cover the cost of _____ copies of *African Openings to the Tree of Life.*

Please send to:

Name _____

Address _____

City, State, Zip _____

Make check payable to **Regent Press** and mail to:

Regent Press
6020-A Adeline
Oakland, CA 94608

To avoid damaging book, please photocopy order form.